Roosevelt Rat's

Learn Magic From A to Z

Discover the Secrets of Real Magicians

Slightly Illusional Publishing
Oregon

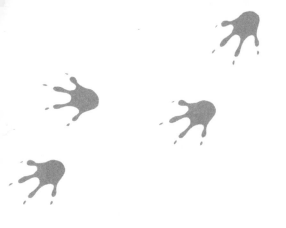

Printed in the United States of America

ISBN 13: 978-0-9816208-0-0

Roosevelt Rat

Contents

Roosevelt Rat's Welcome

Hi there, and thanks for picking up my book. You're probably wondering how a rat could write a book. Well, let me tell you my story. It starts in Miss Patton's first grade classroom. Miss Patton bought a couple rats to be her class pets. (Most teachers buy a turtle or fish, but Miss Patton liked rats. Miss Patton had good taste.)

Miss Patton wanted to reward students who read lots of books, so she called her rats the "Reading Rats." Of course, the rats couldn't read; they were just a reward for reading. Students who read lots of books were allowed to feed the Reading Rats.

Soon those two rats had baby rats. And that's where I come in. Those two rats are my parents. My name is Roosevelt, and I'm a reading rat. And I mean a *reading* rat. Yes, I can read. That's what happens when you spend your whole childhood in Miss Patton's first grade class.

While my brothers and sisters ran on the exercise wheel, I learned my ABC's. While they dug holes, I learned how to put letters together to spell words like "cheese" and "crackers." And while they chased each other's tails, I learned phonics and grammar and vocabulary. Pretty soon I could read and write well enough to start writing my own book.

Then I ran into a problem. My rat claws are made for scavenging for food, not for writing with a pencil. And don't even mention typing—the first sentence in my book came out like this: "Greod fndl psowq v ptywdnm blurt."

But then I met some magicians who travel around to schools and libraries and tells kids about all the great things they can learn by reading books. (Cool job, huh?) I started helping them by doing magic tricks in their shows. The kids loved me. (Of course, everyone loves rats!)

So we became partners. I help in the magic shows and they help me write my books. I **dictate**, which means I tell them what I want to write and they write it down for me. It works out great. That's how we made this book.

Okay, let's jump right into the magic. This book has twenty-six different lessons that teach you how to be a magician. Each lesson explains a different term in magic, like "misdirection." (You can read all about misdirection in the lesson titled "M Is for Misdirection.")

The first lesson features a word that begins with the letter *A*, and the next lesson teaches a *B* word (makes sense, huh?), and the third lesson ... Well, I want you to be surprised.

After explaining what each term means, I'll teach you one of my favorite tricks. Each of these tricks will use the term you just learned. That way, you can learn about magic and then practice what you learned. That will help you remember it longer. And sometimes I'll give you a "star tip." These tips will help you become a star magician. They show you how to take each trick to the next level and do it like a professional would!

After just a few lessons, you'll know a lot about doing magic to entertain your friends and family. By the time you finish the book, you'll be a black belt in rat magic!

You may want to read this book with your parents or a friend. Then you can work together to figure out any tricks that you don't understand. Good luck and happy reading!

Your friend,

Roosevelt Rat

A Is for Accomplice

Usually when you do magic, you work alone. You present a trick and hopefully fool *everyone* watching. Most of the *other* tricks in this book are like that. But the trick in this first lesson is different.

For this trick, you'll work with an accomplice. An **accomplice** is a person in the audience who is secretly helping you. (Or, in my case, another rat that is secretly helping me.) He pretends he's not "in" on the trick, but he really is. The following trick will give you a good idea of how this works.

I "Red" Your Mind

What happens: You leave the room and your friends choose any object in the room. When you return, you're able to guess which object they chose.

What you need: Invite a few friends over to your house and you're ready to go.

Secret: You use an accomplice, of course, and *your accomplice will always point to a red object just before the chosen object.* (That's why the trick is called "I 'Red' Your Mind.") Here's how it works. Wait until you're alone with your best friend or brother. Then explain to him what an accomplice is. Tell him he's going to help you fool your other friends. Make sure he understands that he cannot tell anyone that he's in on the trick.

Then invite a few friends over and explain to them that Roosevelt Rat has taught you how to read minds. Your friends will want you to prove it, so you will. Tell them you will step outside and they can pick any object in the room—a lamp, a pencil, the TV, your cat—and you will identify it when you come back in! After they've picked it, they should call you back in.

When you come back in, your accomplice will start pointing to objects in the room. After each one you'll say, "Nope, that wasn't it" or "Yes, that was it." But how will you know when to say yes? It's easy when you have an accomplice!

Let's say your friends chose your cat as the secret object. Your accomplice might point to a brown pencil first, and you would say, "No, that's not it." Then he would point to the TV, and you would say, "No." Next he might point to a banana, your friend's blue shirt, and then your white wallpaper. You would say no to all of those. Next he would point to your red brick fireplace. That's the signal—a red item! That means the next thing he points to will be the chosen object. So you say no to the fireplace, but you say, "Yes, that's it!" to the next object he points to. Of course, that will be the cat. Make sure your accomplice understands that he needs to point to only one red object and that the chosen object must be the next one he points to.

Of course, everyone will be impressed and want to know how you did it. Don't tell them! That will ruin the whole trick! Offer to do the trick again, but don't tell them how it's done!

Now, you may think using an accomplice is cheating. You may feel like a rat. (Hey! What am I saying? There's nothing wrong with being a rat!) And there's nothing wrong with using an accomplice to trick your friends. It's okay to cheat when you're doing magic.

All magicians cheat when they pull a rabbit out of an empty hat. Of course the hat wasn't *really* empty. They cheated somehow and made it look empty even though it wasn't. Your accomplice is going to help you cheat, just like all the great magicians of the past. Think of it as doing your part to carry on the tradition. (Again, let me say that it's okay to cheat when you're doing magic tricks, but *not* on your school assignments! Don't get those confused!)

Star Tip: Your accomplice can even pretend that he's trying to help your other friends fool you. For example, he can tell them, "Don't stare at the chosen object this time—he must be following your gaze." When you still guess the correct object, he can tell them to all look at the *wrong* object the next time to trick you. Of course, there's nothing they can do to trick you because you're getting the secret clue from your confederate. (A **confederate** is another name for an accomplice—see what a smart rat I am?)

Roosevelt's Favorite Joke #1:
Q: What do rats call a boomerang that won't come back?
A: A stick.

B Is for Blunder

Now we're going to learn what to do when you make a
blunder while doing a magic trick. (A **blunder** is a really big
mistake.) Sooner or later you will make a little boo-boo, like
accidentally showing a card before you're ready. Or maybe
you'll make a serious mistake, like guessing the wrong card.
Or worse yet, a horrible blunder, like dropping all the cards
on the floor in a gigantic pile. (I hate it when I do that! Cards
are so hard to pick up with rat fingers!) When something like
that happens, you'll feel embarrassed. I know I do. *But how
you react is very important to your future as a magician.*

Let's pretend you're doing the "I 'Red' Your Mind" trick from
the last lesson. All your friends are over at your house, and
you decide to show them the trick. Your best friend in the
whole world is your accomplice. You leave the room, then
come back in, and your accomplice starts pointing to objects.
He forgets that red is the secret color and makes you say yes
to the wrong object. Your friends laugh. You feel terrible. You
wish you could hide under a rock. What should you do? Look
at the following options and try to guess which ones are good
reactions and which ones are bad reactions:

Option 1: Yell at your best friend in the whole world.
Tell him it's his fault. Tell him he messed up the
secret signal. Tell him he's fired.

Option 2: Say, "Whoops. I guess I messed that up.
Well, should we go play video games?"

Option 3: Say, "Rats! That was supposed to work.
Well, let me leave the room and you guys choose a
different object …" Then try again.

Option 4: Tell your friends they must have forgotten what they chose, because you did the trick right. Never admit you're wrong! Never!

Well, what do you think? You can probably see that Option 1 and Option 4 are not good. Not good at all. Once you've made a blunder, there is nothing you can do about it. Yelling at your best friend will only make things worse. And refusing to admit your mistake just makes you look silly. Everyone knows you messed up, so admit it and then move on.

That's why Options 2 and 3 are so good. They admit the mistake. Then they suggest another activity so that you don't have to stand there feeling embarrassed.

Here's another idea—if you think people are going to laugh at you, beat them to it. Say something like, "You've heard of the Amazing Houdini? Well, I'm the Amazingly Bad Roosevelt!" (Put your own name in.) If you make a joke about what a bad magician you are, then it won't be very funny if someone else makes a joke about you.

Or you could say, "Don't worry, that's all part of the magic trick." Then in a quiet voice, add, "The part I didn't practice enough." *If you can make fun of yourself and laugh it off, you have just the right personality to be a magician.*

Or finally, you could say, "Well, what do you expect when your magic teacher is a *rat?*" Your friends will say, "What? A rat?" Then you can show them my book. That will take the attention off you, and you won't be as embarrassed.

Of course, we'd rather not make blunders very often. So here's a new trick for you to learn. In this trick, you will show your friends that you can predict the future. (A **prediction** is when you can tell what is going to happen before it happens.) Practice this trick before you show it to anyone, and you will probably do it perfectly. But if you do make a blunder, just laugh it off and start working on your next trick.

Dog-Gone Prediction

What happens: Your friends name some animals that make good pets, and you write those down on slips of paper. One friend chooses one of the animals by pulling its name out of a bag. Then you open your prediction bag and inside is the exact same animal. Somehow you knew what animal your friend would choose!

What you need: Two brown paper lunch bags, a pad of paper, a pen, and a small stuffed dog. A Beanie Baby is about the right size. Put the dog in one of the lunch sacks and then fold over the top and tape it closed. Write "Prediction" on the bag with a marker. (You could use any kind of stuffed animal, but I'll describe the trick using a dog. Of course, a rat would be best, but for some reason rats aren't very popular with toy makers. Go figure.)

Secret: *You actually write "dogs" on every piece of paper.* Here's how it works. First, get together a group of friends and tell them you can predict the future. Then say, "Let me demonstrate."

Ask your friends to call out some kinds of animals that make good pets. They will probably say dogs, cats, birds, hamsters, rabbits, and more. (Your smarter friends will also mention rats.) As they call out each name, you pretend to write it on a piece of paper and drop it into the empty lunch bag.

But instead of each animal name, you write the same thing on every piece of paper. So when they say "dogs," you write "dogs," and drop it in the lunch bag. When they say "cats," you write, "dogs," and drop it in the bag. When they say "hamsters," you write "dogs." Get the idea?

Drop about seven or eight papers into the first bag. Then call attention to your prediction bag—the one with the stuffed animal in it. Tell your friends that you made a prediction about what animal they would pick. Tell them, "I can only see about a day into the future, so yesterday I predicted which of these animals you would choose. Let's see if I was right."

Then ask one of your friends to reach into the other bag and pull out a piece of paper. Tell him to do it without looking at the papers. (He can't look because you don't want him to see that all the slips of paper say "dogs." You may want to hold the bag up for him, so that he can't see down into it.)

When he pulls out a slip of paper, ask him to read it out loud to everyone. Naturally, he will say "dogs." Then ask another friend to rip open your prediction bag and show everyone the prediction. Of course, it will also be a dog. You're amazing. Take a bow and throw away both bags immediately. (You don't want anyone to examine the slips of paper!)

Star Tip: Remember, don't tell your friends how to do the trick, no matter how much they beg. And if you make a mistake during this trick, just laugh about it. Maybe you can say, "Well, if I really could predict the future, then I would have known I was going to mess up that trick!"

Roosevelt's Favorite Joke #2:
Q: What should a slow rat eat before a race?
A: Ketchup.

C Is for Clean

Have you tried the "Dog-Gone Prediction" trick yet? I hope so. If not, try it! But when you're done, make sure you get rid of the bag of papers that all say "dog." If people see those slips, they'll know how you did the trick. And that's no fun.

Magicians say the slips are **gimmicked**. That means there's something tricky about them—something that the magician doesn't want the audience to know about. The magician has to get rid of the slips before anyone can examine them. Magicians call that **ditching** them. So if you hang around magicians, you'll probably hear them talk about "ditching the gimmick."

When you've ditched the gimmick, you're **clean**. *Magicians like to be clean.* Clean is good. That's why "C Is for Clean" is the title of this magic lesson.

Tricks that don't use gimmicks are nice because there is nothing to ditch. The audience can examine everything to their hearts' content. You finish the trick clean. Let's learn a trick that doesn't use any gimmicks, so that you too can be squeaky-clean.

"Have To" Make Money

What happens: You show a dollar bill and you show that both your hands are empty. Then you fold up the dollar bill and put it in a friend's hand. You make a corny joke, and your friend opens the dollar to find a half-dollar inside!

What you need: A dollar bill and a half-dollar coin. That's it. No gimmicks. You're clean.

Secret: *You use a clever method of hiding the half-dollar until you reveal it at the end.* Here's how you do it. Take the dollar and coin out of your pocket and hold them like this:

Here's what it looks like to your friend:

Say, "See this dollar? Since we're kids, dollars are just for fun." Let go of the dollar with your left fingers, and point to it with your left hand. This shows that your left hand is empty. It looks like this from your view:

Then say, "But adults always seem to worry about money, like they're not going to have enough." Illustrate this by scrunching the dollar together. As you do, you can grab the coin with your left thumb and fingers, like this:

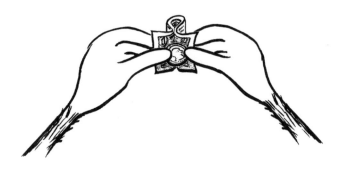

Then say, "But adults always seem to be able to stretch their money and buy everything they need." As you say this, stretch the dollar bill back out but hold onto the coin with the left thumb. Now it will look like this to you:

Say, "So there's nothing to worry about." As you say this, point to the dollar with the right hand. This shows the right hand is also empty. So now you've shown a dollar bill and two empty hands. Your friend will believe that you don't have anything else in your hands.

Now wrap the dollar bill around the half-dollar without letting your friend see the coin. To do this, hold your left hand still and wrap around it with your right hand, as shown in the next picture:

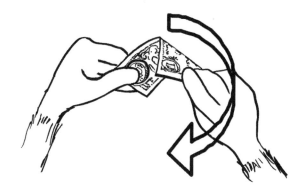

Then grab the whole bundle and squeeze it tightly and place it in your friend's hand. Close his fingers around it. Tell him, "Some day, you'll have a family, and you'll have to make money. You'll *have to.*" Then take the dollar bill back, unroll it, and show the half-dollar coin.

Say, "A dollar bill and a *half, too.* Get it? You'll 'have to' make money ... A dollar bill and a 'half, too ...' A half-dollar ... Oh, never mind."

Your friend probably won't like the joke, but hey—what do you expect? This is *Roosevelt Rat's Learn Magic from A to Z,* not *Roosevelt Rat's Big Book of Jokes.* (Although that sounds like a good idea. Maybe I'll work on that next.) Speaking of jokes ...

Roosevelt's Favorite Joke #3:
Q: Do rats stir their hot chocolate with their right hand or left hand?
A: Neither, they use their spoon.

D Is for Delay

In the "'Have To' Make Money" trick, why did you put the dollar in your friend's hand? Why not just show the dollar bill and then turn it around to reveal the coin? I'll tell you why: *the trick is better when your friend thinks the coin appeared right in his own hand.*

That's a good example of using a delay. To **delay** means to leave some time between when you do your secret move and when you reveal the surprise. The surprise is also called the **revelation**. (See "R Is for Revelation" for more about making a revelation exciting.) So it's a good idea to "delay the revelation" in your magic tricks.

In the "'Have To' Make Money" trick, the secret move is done when you switch the half-dollar from your right thumb to your left thumb. That's how you hide the coin and show that both of your hands are empty. Then you put the bill in your friend's hand and tell your silly joke. That's the delay. Then you finish the silly joke as you reveal the half-dollar. That's the revelation. Let's learn another trick that uses a delay.

Floating Cards

What happens: You let two friends each hide a card somewhere in the deck. Then you magically cause the cards to float to the top of the deck.

What you need: Just a deck of cards.

Secret: The cards don't really float to the top of the deck. *The cards at the top of the deck are similar to, but not exactly the same, as the cards your friends hide in the middle of the deck.*

Before your friends come over, take the 6 of clubs and the 9 of spades out of the deck and keep them handy. (If you don't know, the clubs are black and look like three-leaf clovers. Spades are also black, but they look like an upside-down heart or a pointy shovel.)

Then take out two cards that look almost the same— the 9 of clubs and the 6 of spades—and put them on top of the **face-down deck**. A face-down deck means that the face of the cards, the side with the numbers and the pictures, is facing down. The back of the cards, the side with the blue or red design, is facing up. Now you're all set. Invite some friends over.

When your friends arrive, tell them, "Magicians are always making things float. Sometimes they even float a lady from the audience. Since I'm just learning magic, I'm going to float something easier. How about these two cards?" Then show your friends the 6 of clubs and the 9 of spades.

Don't call a lot of attention to these cards. Don't even name them. Just hold them up so your friends can see them. Then give the cards to your friends. Hold the rest of the deck in your hand, face down. Have your friends slide their cards somewhere in the middle of the deck.

Then tell them, "This is where I make the cards float to the top." Slowly shake the whole deck from side to side. Frown and pretend it's not working. Ask them to repeat the magic words after you: "Rats Rule!" (You can use whatever magic words you want, but I highly recommend "Rats Rule!") Frown and pretend that didn't work either. Finally, say, "Okay, I'll just have to sneak up on them."

Then bring your other hand down on top of the deck as quick and hard as you can. Give the deck a good slap. That doesn't really do anything, but it looks impressive. Then turn over the top two cards and show your friends that their cards "floated" to the top.

Now, you and I know that the top two cards aren't *exactly* your friends' cards. But your friends probably won't notice the difference. If they do, refer to "B Is for Blunder." Remember to be a good sport and just laugh about it. Congratulate your friends on having a great memory. Tell them very few people notice that they aren't the exact same cards. But chances are they won't notice and they'll be very impressed.

Star Tip: Now think about this—you could have had them put the cards in the deck then immediately turned over the top two cards. You could have skipped all that stuff with the shaking and saying the magic words and slapping the deck. But then the trick is too obvious. There's no way you could have gotten their cards to the top of the deck that quickly. So your friends might have suspected the top cards weren't really theirs. It's much better to put the delay in. Let them wonder *when and how* you "moved" their cards to the top.

Roosevelt's Favorite Joke #4:
Q: Why do cowboys ride horses?
A: Because they're too heavy to carry.

E Is for Effect

Magicians don't do tricks. Well, they do tricks, but they don't call them tricks. Magicians call them **effects**. So instead of saying, "I love the 'Floating Lady' *trick*," a magician would say, "I love the 'Floating Lady' *effect*." The **effect** is what the audience sees. The **trick** is what the magician does that the audience doesn't see.

In "Dog-Gone Prediction," the *effect* is predicting the animal that your friend will choose. The *trick* is writing the same word on all the slips. In "'Have To' Make Money," the *effect* is making a coin appear inside a dollar bill. The *trick* is hiding it until it is revealed.

Now we're going to learn an effect called "Hungry Hippo." As you read about it, try to figure out what the effect is and what the trick is.

Hungry Hippo

What happens: A friend marks a quarter and you put it in your pocket. It magically appears under a picture of a hippo.

What you need: A quarter, a marker, and a picture of a hippo. Take a picture of your pet hippo, or, if you don't have a hippo, print a hippo picture from the Internet or draw one yourself. Place the quarter, tails up, under the hippo picture. Now you're ready to begin.

Secret: *You use two quarters.* You borrow one from a friend and you have a different quarter sitting under the hippo picture the whole time. That quarter is called a **duplicate** quarter. That means it looks exactly like the quarter you borrowed from your friend. Here's how you use it.

First, ask to borrow a quarter from your friend. Hand her the marker and hold out the quarter with heads facing up. Ask her to mark her quarter with a cross, a smiley face, or her initials. Then drop the quarter into your right pocket as you say, "I'm going to put your money in my pocket so my hungry hippo doesn't eat it."

Point to the hippo picture and tell your friend, "Hippos eat 250 pounds of grass a day. That's a quarter of a … Oh, wait a minute. Did I just say a quarter?" Reach back into your pocket and pretend to feel around for her marked quarter. Act like it's not there. You and I know the quarter is still in your pocket, but your friend doesn't, so make it look convincing.

Then act frustrated with your hippo. Yell at the picture, "You ate another quarter? You naughty hungry hippo!" Lift the picture up and show the duplicate quarter under the picture. Again, you and I know it's not really her quarter, but your friend doesn't. She'll naturally assume it is her quarter. (Remember, it's tails up, and the mark she put on her quarter was on heads.)

Quickly take the duplicate quarter and drop it into your pocket and say to your friend, "Well, thanks for the quarter!" Smile, then say, "Just kidding." Leave the duplicate quarter in your pocket and pull out her marked quarter and hand it back. She'll never know that two quarters were used.

Pop Quiz: What do you think was the *effect* and what was the *trick*? The effect was making a quarter appear under a picture. And the trick was you were using a duplicate quarter. Excellent! Keep up the good work. Now go try this effect on a friend or a family member.

Roosevelt's Favorite Joke #5:
Q: What do rats in Australia call little black cats?
A: Kittens.

F Is for Flash

In the last lesson, you learned how to make a quarter appear by using a duplicate. Throughout the whole effect, the audience only sees one quarter at a time, so there's no reason for them to suspect you're using two quarters.

But what would happen if you accidentally let them glimpse both quarters at the same time? It would ruin the effect! When a magician accidentally shows something he's supposed to be hiding, that's called **flashing**. For example, if your audience sees the duplicate quarter before you put the original quarter in your pocket—you flashed the duplicate quarter. You should practice each effect until you're pretty sure you won't flash. (But if you do, see "B Is for Blunder" for how to handle it.)

Okay, let's learn a new trick. This is a great effect, so have fun with it. Just try not to flash.

Rat Survivor

What happens: You place a mark on one side of five coins and give them to your friend. She tosses them onto a table. The coins that land with the mark showing "survive," and the other ones are "voted off the island." You keep doing this until only one coin is left. The final survivor turns out to be the coin that you predicted!

What you need: Five coins. They can be a mixture of pennies, nickels, dimes, or quarters. And you need a marker. And you need a prediction card. Personally, I would draw a handsome rat like me, Roosevelt, on a piece of paper. Fold the paper up and write "prediction" on it.

Secret: *One coin has a mark on both sides, so it survives each round no matter which side it lands on.* That coin will be the one you predict will win. When your friend isn't watching, write an *R* on the back of one coin and put it in your hand with the other four coins. Hold some of the coins heads up, and some tails up, but make sure the *R* is facing down so your friend can't see it. In other words, don't flash the *R* on the gimmicked coin. And remember which coin has the *R* on the back! It should look like this to your friend:

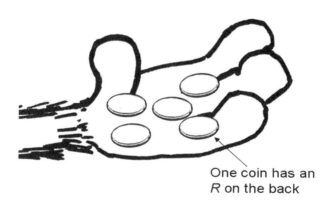

One coin has an
R on the back

To start the effect, ask your friend if she's heard of the TV show *Survivor.* Tell her that the animals decided to have their own *Survivor* competition. A lot of animals tried out for the show, but they only accepted a dog, a hog, a frog, a cat, and a rat. As you name the animals, write the first letter of their name on one of the coins—*D* for dog, then *H* for hog, *F* for frog, *C* for cat, and *R* for rat. Make sure you write the *R* on the back of the gimmicked coin that already has an *R* on the other side. Now it has an *R* on both sides and can't be eliminated, no matter which side lands facing up during the game. Now it looks like this:

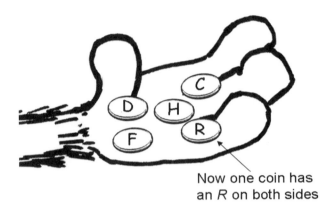

Now one coin has
an *R* on both sides

Tell your friend that you know who will win the competition and that you wrote your prediction on the piece of paper that says "prediction."

Then drop the coins in a paper cup and tell your friend that she is going to be in charge of the competition. For each round of animal *Survivor*, she'll dump all the coins out onto the table. Then she'll say, "You've been voted off the island" as she removes the coins that do not have their letter showing. Keep doing this until only one coin is left. As you know, that will be the rat.

Explain that you knew the rat would win because rats are so smart, so cute, and so perfect in every way. (Well, I think so!) Ask her to check your prediction paper. While she opens the paper, you can take all the coins and drop them in your pocket. Remember, you don't want her to see the back of the gimmicked coin. Be careful not to flash it as you put it away.

Star Tip: If you really want to be tricky, you can have another coin in your pocket that has just one *R* on it. While your friend checks the prediction paper, you can switch that coin with the gimmicked two-*R* coin. Now your friend can examine all the coins. In other words, you ditched the gimmick without flashing it and now you're clean. Wow, that sentence used four magical terms, and you've learned them all! You're well on your way to being a real magician. Give yourself a pat on the back and tell yourself that you're one of Roosevelt's best students!

Roosevelt's Favorite Joke #6:
Q: What do sharks like to eat?
A: Peanut butter and jellyfish sandwiches.

G Is for Gimmick

I know, I know—we've already talked about **gimmicks**. But gimmicks are so important to magicians that I thought they deserved their own lesson. There are gimmicks that help you float people on stage, saw a woman in half, link rings together, and even pour water out of your ear!

But sometimes simple gimmicks are the best. For example, the gimmick in the next effect is just a pad of paper. This is a good effect to perform for your class at school. You need a crowd for this one. Don't do it for just a few friends. You'll see why …

It All Adds Up

What happens: Three people in your class write a number on a pad of paper. You ask a fourth person to add them up and call out the answer. Then you open your hand and reveal the same number written on your palm.

What you need: A pad of paper like the one shown in the drawing on the next page. Open it to about the middle. The front piece of paper is blank. Turn the pad over to the back and write the following three numbers in pencil: 213, 799, and 501. Try to write each one in slightly different handwriting. For example, write one big, one messy, and one normal. Turn it back to the front side so the numbers are hidden. Now your pad is gimmicked. You also need to have a pencil and calculator with you. And you need to write 1513 on your hand. See the drawings below for how to "gimmick" the pad.

The pad looks like this on the front:

It has these numbers hidden on the back:

Secret: *The numbers that will be added up on the calculator are the ones that you wrote on the pad earlier.* So of course the answer matches what you wrote on your hand.

Here's how you use the gimmicked pad. Take the pad, calculator, and pencil to class. When your teacher gives you permission, tell the class that you will now demonstrate that math is easy and fun. Hand the pencil to a person on the left side of the class and ask him to write a three-digit number, like 207, on the pad. Hold the pad out to him and keep holding it while he writes on it. (That way he can't turn it over and see the numbers you wrote on the back.)

Then move back a couple desks and ask another person to do the same. Then move over a row and ask a third person to write down another three-digit number. Then go to your desk to get the calculator. Before you pick up the calculator, switch the pad to your left hand. This will automatically turn the pad over. In other words, now the numbers that you wrote are facing up and the numbers your friends wrote are facing down, hidden in the palm of your left hand.

Then walk to the opposite side of the classroom and hand the calculator to another person. (You move to the opposite side of the room so that the number writers won't be able to see that the numbers have been switched.) Ask the person to add up the three numbers. You don't hand the pad to her, for the same reason as before—you don't want her to turn it over and see the second set of numbers. When the person with the calculator finishes adding the numbers up, ask her what the total is. She'll say, "1513."

Then you say, "See, math is fun and easy. Somehow, I just knew it would all add up." Open your hand to show that you predicted that 1513 would be the answer. While everyone is looking at your hand, put the gimmicked pad in your pocket with your other hand. There, you just ditched the gimmick. You're a true magician. You're doing great. I'd say you've earned your orange belt in rat magic.

Roosevelt's Favorite Joke #7:
Q: What kind of bee can't make up its mind?
A: A may-bee.

H Is for Humor

It's fun doing magic tricks to amaze your friends. It's even more fun if you add **humor** and make your friends laugh, too. One of my favorite tricks isn't really a trick at all—it's just a silly gag. A **gag** is a joke that uses some object to make it funny. In this case, the object is a stuffed animal.

And in this gag, you actually reveal the secret of the trick. I know, I know—that's against the rules! But in this case we'll allow it because it's so funny.

The Flying Giraffe

What happens: You display a stuffed animal on the floor, hold a blanket up in front of it, and it begins floating above the top of the blanket.

What You Need: A blanket, an accomplice, and a stuffed animal. It doesn't actually have to be a stuffed animal. You can float anything you want in this trick. I like to float cookies. I float them right into my mouth. But that's a different effect.

Secret: *Your accomplice makes the animal float.* In this effect, the audience must not know about the accomplice. So before the effect begins, have your accomplice hide behind a couch. Then ask your parents to come in and sit down in the family room. Place the stuffed animal on the floor, near the edge of the couch that your accomplice is hiding behind.

Ask your parents if they've heard of flying fish. Tell them, "Flying fish don't really fly, they just jump out of the water. Flying fish can't fly, and neither can giraffes. Except this one—this giraffe can fly." (If you're not using a giraffe, change the wording. For example, say, "Spiderman action figures can't fly either. Except this one.")

Then hold the blanket up in front of the giraffe, hiding it from your parents. Also, make sure the blanket covers the edge of the couch, so that your accomplice can sneak out without being seen. Then you'll be standing by the couch, holding a curtain that hides your giraffe and your accomplice from your parents. The following picture shows you what it should look like:

Your accomplice sneaks out from behind the couch.

39

Now your accomplice can lift the giraffe up so that his head is peeking over the blanket (the giraffe's head, not your accomplice's). Then he can make the giraffe "walk" back and forth while peeking over the curtain. This is what it looks like from the front:

He can even toss it up in the air so it flies above the curtain and drops back down behind it again. Finally, when you think your parents are totally impressed, step back and take a deep bow. "Accidentally" pull the curtain away, showing your best friend.

Your parents will crack up when they see your best friend behind the curtain and realize he was holding the giraffe up. You can act embarrassed, like that wasn't supposed to happen. Trust me—it's hysterical.

One of my rat friends laughed so hard he had the hiccups for weeks! Try it and see if you can crack your parents up.

Roosevelt's Favorite Joke #8:
Q: What does a rat become after he's three days old?
A: Four days old.

And since this lesson is all about humor, here's a bonus joke for you ...

Roosevelt's Bonus Joke of the Day:
Q: How can you tell which end of a worm is its head?
A: Tickle it in the middle and see which end laughs.

I Is for Impromptu

An **impromptu** trick is one that can be done anytime, anywhere. An impromptu trick uses common objects like coins or napkins. Impromptu tricks are very handy when you're at a friend's house and he asks you to show him an effect. You probably won't have any gimmicks ready, so it's nice to know an impromptu trick, like this one.

Two-for-One Deal

What happens: You and a friend take turns eliminating coins from a pile. Eventually, one coin will be left after all the others have been eliminated. Then you reveal your prediction. You predicted the exact coin that is left!

What You Need: Eight borrowed coins. They can be a mixture of pennies, nickels, dimes, quarters, or half-dollars. Using a permanent marker, number the coins on one side from 1 to 8. Write "Coin 2 is the best deal" on a piece of paper. Don't let your friends see what you wrote on the paper. Fold it up and give it to one of your friends to hold.

Secret: *You use the "two-for-one" idea to make sure that the coin you predicted is the last coin left.* Here's how it works. After you've labeled the coins, spread them out on a table with the numbers facing up. Pick one of your friends to help with the trick, and explain that you're going to take turns eliminating coins. Tell him, "This trick is called the 'Two-for-One Deal.' You'll point to two coins, and I'll choose which one to remove. Then I'll point to two coins, and you'll choose which one to remove. We'll keep doing that until only one coin is left."

Let your friend point to two coins. (Your friend has to go first for this trick. If you go first, it won't work.) Suppose he points to coin 1 and coin 4. You can remove either one, because it's coin 2 that you predicted would be left.

Then you point to two coins. They can be any two coins *except* coin 2! For example, you might point to coin 3 and coin 5. Then your friend goes again. Suppose he points to coin 2 and coin 8. Remember, your prediction is that coin 2 will be left, so you do not want to remove 2! Therefore, you calmly tell him to remove coin 8.

On your turn, you never point to coin 2, so your friend never gets the chance to remove it. On his turn, if he points to coin 2 as one of his two choices, you always pick the other coin. You keep doing this until coin 2 is the only coin left.

Then you ask the person holding your prediction to read what you wrote. He'll unfold it and read, "Coin 2 is the best deal." Everyone will wonder how you predicted that would be the last coin. Let them wonder.

Roosevelt's Favorite Joke #9:
Q: What did the rat say to the man with three heads?
A: Hello, hello, hello.

43

J Is for Just for Fun

Some effects are really impressive—like the "Two-for-One Deal," where you predict the one coin that will be left. Well, the effects in this lesson are not that impressive, but they are fun. I call them "Just for Fun" effects, and here's a couple for you to try out on your friends.

Magical Pen

What happens: Your pen magically writes any color that your friend names.

What You Need: A pen and a piece of paper.

Secret: Start by pulling a pen out of your backpack. Hold it up to your friend and say, "This is my new magic color pen. It will write any color you want."

Your friend probably won't believe you, so bet her a dollar that it can write any color she wants. Suppose she says, "Green." Then you write G-R-E-E-N on the piece of paper. Say, "See, it wrote 'GREEN'! I told you it could write any color."

Your friend assumed that you meant your pen could write *in* blue ink or *in* red ink. But actually you only said that it can *write* any color, not write *in* any color. You win a dollar, which you can use for the next effect. (Be sure to give your friend her dollar back when you're done, or you might lose a friend. Believe me—friends are worth more than money.)

Unbeatable Gravity

What happens: You drop a dollar bill and your friend can never catch it.

What You Need: A dollar bill. Simple, huh?

Secret: You hold the dollar bill lightly at the top edge. Position your friend's hand near the bottom of the bill, like this:

Here's a close up showing exactly how each person's hands should be positioned:

Tell your friend you're going to let go of the bill and she's supposed to close her fingers and catch it. Wait a couple seconds, then let go. She won't be able to catch it. You can let her try as many times as she wants, but she won't be able to do it.

Reaction time makes this trick work. **Reaction time** is the amount of time it takes to react to a stimulus. (A **stimulus** is something that causes your friend to take action.) In this case, your friend is watching to see when you let go of the dollar bill. That's the stimulus. That tells her to begin closing her fingers. However, there's a delay between you dropping the bill and her closing her fingers. That delay is her reaction time. It takes her brain a second to figure out what it's seeing and to send a message to her fingers to close. That's why she can't catch it.

However, if you try to catch the bill yourself, you can catch it every time. That's because your brain already knows when you're going to drop it. Your brain doesn't have to react to a stimulus, so there is no reaction time.

Roosevelt's Favorite Joke #10:
Q: What is furry and cute and has sixteen wheels?
A: A rat on Rollerblades.

K Is for Key Card

Well, you've made it through ten lessons of *Roosevelt Rat's Learn Magic From A to Z*. I hope you're enjoying this course on magic. And I really hope you've tried a few of these effects out on your family and friends. As you do these effects, try to present them in a fun way. The real magic isn't being able to fool people. *The real magic is being able to entertain people.* In other words, try to make your effects funny and interesting. If you do, everyone will enjoy them.

For example, this effect uses a key card. A **key card** is a card that helps you find the card that someone else chooses. I'll explain how that works soon. But as you read through this trick, notice that the presentation is what makes it really fun. After all, who wouldn't want to watch an effect that features the world's smartest rat?

World's Smartest Rat

What happens: Your pet rat does a card trick. If you don't have a rat, any kind of pet will work—dog, hamster, snake, goldfish, alligator, hippo. If you don't have any pets, draw a picture of a rat and call that the world's smartest rat.

That's Me!

What You Need: A deck of cards and a pet or a drawing of a pet.

Secret: *You use a key card to find the card your friend chose.* Here's how it works. Hand your friend a deck of cards and ask her to choose one card. Take the rest of the deck back from her and say, "Don't let me see your card, and definitely don't show it to my rat, Roosevelt!" Now you really have her attention.

Say, "Roosevelt is the world's smartest rat. Yes, it's true. He's so smart he writes books, composes music, and he even does card tricks. See, here's a regular deck …" As you say this, spread the deck open like this:

You pretend to be doing this to convince your friend the deck is a regular deck. However, you're actually spreading the cards out so you can get a peek at the bottom card. The bottom card is the key card in this trick. In the picture above, it's the 2 of hearts. Remember that card.

Then turn the deck facedown and have your friend put her card on top, like this:

Then say, "Now we'll lose your card somewhere in this deck so that Roosevelt will have no idea what card you chose." Pull off about half of the top of the deck, and put the bottom half on top of it, as shown below:

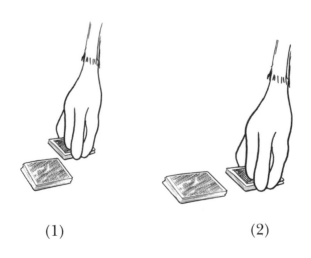

(1)   (2)

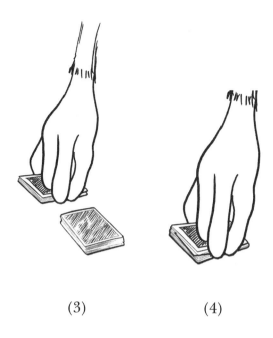

(3)   (4)

When you do this, it puts the key card right on top
of the card your friend chose. Sneaky, huh? Then
spread the cards out on the table faceup, like this:

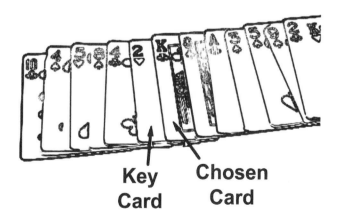

**Key   Chosen
Card   Card**

Review what's happened so far. Say, "You chose a card from the deck. You didn't show it to Roosevelt or me. Then you put the card back and we hid it somewhere in the middle of the deck. It would be impossible for anyone to guess your card ... unless you're dealing with the world's smartest rat. Just to prove his incredible intelligence to you, he will now pick up your card and hand it to you!"

Look at your rat and wait for him to do something. Of course, he won't even try to find the card. He could care less about the cards. (Unless you're dealing with the real Roosevelt, rat magician *numero uno*!) Act like you're waiting for him to do the trick. Smile like you're embarrassed that he's not doing anything. Then bend down to the rat and put your ear right in front of his mouth. Pretend that he's whispering to you. Nod your head and say, "Uh-huh … Oh, I see … Okay."

Turn to your friend and say, "He told me which card is yours. I don't know how he knows, but he said it was this one." Reach down and pick up the card that is on top of the key card. It will be the card your friend chose. Hand it to her and give the world's smartest rat a cookie.

Roosevelt's Favorite Joke #11:
Q: How does an alien count to twenty-three?
A: On his fingers.

L Is for Levitation

Levitation—now there's a fancy term for you. See if you can pick out the correct definition from the following choices.

    A. Collecting levies or taxes from citizens.

    B. Floating an object in the air.

    C. The sound a hamster makes when it burps.

If you chose *B,* you were right. **Levitation** is floating an object in the air. And that's impressive, because it breaks the law of gravity. So, if you can levitate an object, you are a magician, no doubt about it.

Let's learn an easy levitation trick.

Up, Up, and Away

What happens: A card floats off the top of a deck as you wave your hand over it.

What You Need: A deck of Go Fish cards, with pictures of animals, and a glue stick—the little tube of glue that rubs on purple and then turns clear when it dries. Rub a little glue on your right thumb and right middle finger before you start the effect.

Secret: Since gravity is everywhere, all levitation tricks work the same—*something that the audience can't see is used to "float" the object.* Sometimes it's a string, but for our trick we'll use a little glue.

Hold the deck in your left hand with the pictures face up. I'll assume the octopus is the face-up card, but you can change the story to fit whichever picture you want to use.

Here is the story using an octopus: "Superman had lots of powers, such as X-ray vision, superhuman strength, and the ability to fly. What caused these superpowers? Well, as everyone knows, he's from the planet Krypton. This octopus, whose name happens to be Clark, is also from the planet Krypton. Here, I'll prove it to you. He has X-ray vision. See? Right now Clark is looking through the ceiling and counting the clouds in the sky. You don't believe me? Okay, well how about a demonstration of his flying powers?"

At this point, place your right hand on the octopus card. Press your thumb and middle finger against the card so that the glue sticks to the card. Then slowly raise the card about an inch off the deck, as shown on the next page.

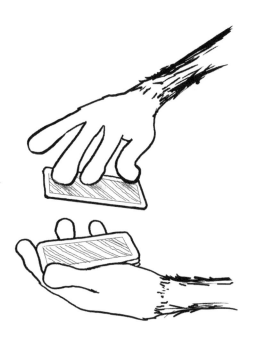

When you reach about an inch high, yell, "Oh no! Kryptonite! Losing power … Can't fly much longer …" and lower the card back onto the deck.

Now use your left thumb to hold down the top card while you pull your right hand away. This is how you unstick your fingers from the card.

Notice that you only want to levitate the card for a couple seconds. Why not longer? Because the longer you levitate it, the longer your audience has to figure out how you're doing it. It's better to finish quickly and leave them wondering.

M Is for Misdirection

Sometimes a magician will make a coin disappear and he'll say, "The hand is quicker than the eye." In other words, he wants you to believe he moved his hand so quickly that you couldn't see him put the coin away. Don't believe him.

Actually, the eye is quicker than the hand. Here, let me show you. Grab a napkin from your kitchen. Crumple it up into a ball and hold it in your open left hand. Now, try to grab the napkin with your right hand and put it in your pocket so fast that nobody could see you do it. Did you try it? How did it work? Not very well, I'll bet, because the *eye* is quicker than the *hand*.

That's why magicians have to use misdirection. **Misdirection** is distracting people so they don't see what you're doing. For example, you get them to look at your right hand so that your left hand can do the secret move.

Of course, you can't say, "Look at my right hand!" If you say that, people will know you're trying to trick them, and they'll watch your left hand instead. So you have to be less obvious. The best way to get them to look where you want is by using your eyes. If you stare at your right hand, they'll look at your right hand. Another trick is moving your right hand. Your audience will naturally watch the hand that is moving and ignore your other hand.

Remember, once you get good at misdirection, you'll be able to do almost anything in magic, even eat a napkin! (Some people may be asking why you would *want* to eat a napkin. Good question. I guess us rats will eat anything.)

The Yummy Napkin

What happens: You eat a napkin! (Not really, but that's what it looks like.)

What You Need: A napkin. And some misdirection.

Secret: *You trick your family into watching your right hand instead of your left hand.* Here's how. Try this effect at dinnertime. Say, "Thanks for dinner, Mom. It's delicious!" (This is a good thing to say even if you're not doing a trick. Your mom works hard to make that dinner, so thank her for it!) Then say, "And the napkins are tasty, too!"

Your mom will probably be surprised that you think the napkins are tasty. You can say, "Oh, you haven't tried yours? Look, they're delicious." Then take your paper napkin in your left hand and crumple it up into a ball like this:

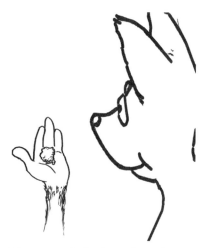

Reach over with your right hand and pretend to pick

the napkin up with your right fingers, but really leave it in your left hand. At the same time, close your left hand around the napkin and drop your hand down below the table. See the pictures below:

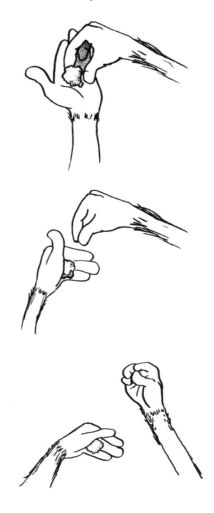

You should practice that move in front of a mirror. Try doing it once and really taking the napkin in the right hand. Then try it again but actually leave the napkin in your left hand. See if you can make it look the same as the time when you really did take the napkin.

Once you've got that down, practice adding misdirection. As your right hand comes away from your left, stare at your right hand. Act like the napkin is really there. At the same time, you drop your left hand into your lap and just leave the napkin there. Completely ignore your left hand while you stare at your right. Then bring your right hand up to your lips and slowly pretend to put the napkin in your mouth. Pretend to chew on the napkin. Then swallow like you're swallowing a big wad of napkin. Lastly, say, "Mmmm, delicious! Almost as good as your dinner, Mom."

Roosevelt's Favorite Joke #13:
Q: What animal has two humps and is found at the North Pole?
A: A lost camel.

N Is for Never Reveal the Secret

If you've been trying the tricks in this book, I bet you've already been asked, "How did you do that?" So let me tell you a little secret: Most people don't really want to know how the trick is done. They're just giving you a compliment. When they say, "How did you do that?" they really mean, "Wow, what a great effect!"

So how should you answer when people ask, "How did you do that?" You can try any of these answers:

- Did you like that? Thanks!
- That was cool, huh?
- Yeah, I love that effect too.
- Oh, I learned that from Roosevelt Rat. You should check out that crazy rat's Website.

Other people really do want to know how the trick is done, but they will almost always be disappointed if you tell them. After they learn the secret, they will say, "That's it? You just drop the napkin in your lap? That's so simple!" So remember, no matter how much they beg you, you can't tell them how the trick is done.

So what do you do if they just keep asking and asking? Well, it's good to have one trick that you don't mind teaching to your friends. It should be a trick that doesn't give away any big magic secrets. A good example would be the "Flying Giraffe" effect from "H Is for Humor." Teach them how to do that trick so they can go home and show their parents. Letting them in on one of your secrets will be fun for all of you, giving you something cool to share.

So learn the following effect and use it to amaze and entertain your friends, but don't reveal the secret!

Flipped-Out Coin

What happens: You toss a coin in the air and it disappears.

What You Need: A quarter and a lucky rock. Actually, it doesn't even have to be that lucky.

Secret: This trick is similar to the napkin trick; *it's all based on misdirection.* Here's how it works. Put the quarter and the lucky rock in your left pants pocket. Then, when you and your friend are trying to decide what to play next, offer to flip a coin to decide. Pull the quarter out of your pocket and hold it in your open left hand. Then reach over with your right hand and pretend to take it just like you did in the "Yummy Napkin" effect. At the same time, close your left fingers to hide the quarter in your left hand.

Now your friend thinks you're holding a quarter in your right hand. Tell him you're going to wave your lucky rock over the coin. With your left hand, reach into your pocket and pull out the lucky rock. As you reach into your pocket for the rock, leave the quarter in your pocket. Now it has completely disappeared, although your friend doesn't know it yet. That was easy, huh?

Wave the lucky rock over the quarter you're

pretending to hold in your right hand. Tell your friend, "This lucky rock magic-izes the quarter so it always makes the right choice. Unless I give it too much magic, then sometimes it just flips out." Pretend to flip the coin in the air and act like you're waiting for it to come down. To your friend it seems to have vanished into thin air. Say, "Well, I guess it really did flip out. Well, let's go have some cookies."

Star Tip: If your friends really seem interested in learning magic, it's okay to start teaching them more of the secrets. The general rule is that magicians will teach a friend how to do a trick only if the friend really wants to perform the effect for other people. We will not teach someone a trick just because he or she wants to know the secret.

Roosevelt's Favorite Joke #14:
Q: Why are short pencils bad?
A: Because they can never be-long to you.

O Is for Outs

Today I'm going to share with you one of the first effects I ever learned. But don't think it's a boring trick just for beginners. Many of the magicians I work with still use this effect in programs they present to thousands of students every year.

Here's how it works. You let your friend choose from three different items, and she will always pick the one you wanted her to pick. Sounds impossible, doesn't it? It was impossible until some smart magician invented "outs."

Outs mean that your friend can choose any item and you have a way "out." In other words, you have a different plan for each choice your friend can make. If she chooses the first item, you go with plan 1. If she chooses the second item, you switch to plan 2. And finally, the third item leads to plan 3.

Let me show you how it works in this next trick.

The Smart Cookie Test

What happens: Your friend chooses a color. She always chooses the color that "smarties" choose.

What You Need: Three pieces of construction paper, each a different color. Let's say the colors are red, purple, and blue. Write "Smarties always choose blue" on the back of the blue paper. Write lightly so that it doesn't show through from the other side. Don't write anything on the red and purple papers.

You also need a folder to keep the papers in. On the inside of the folder, write "Smarties always choose red." And you need a magic pointer. To make the pointer, write "Smarties always choose purple" on a piece of blank paper. Then roll the paper up with the writing on the inside so it looks like a straw. Put a piece of tape on it to keep it rolled up. Okay, now you're ready.

Secret: *You use outs to make it look like your friend always chooses the right color.* First, explain to your friend that there is one color that smarties always choose. Then take the papers out of the folder. Be careful not to flash the writing on the inside of the folder or the writing on the back of the blue card. Put the cards on the table and hand your friend the pointer. Ask her to point to one of the three colors.

If she points to the blue paper, then you're in luck. That's the easiest. Just tell her to turn the blue paper over and see if she's a smartie. After she turns the blue paper over, she'll probably think you wrote the same thing on the back of all the papers. Let her turn the other papers over and she'll be amazed that they're blank. Remember, never reveal the secret.

But what if she chooses red? Well, don't worry, you have an out. If that happens, you switch to plan 2. Instead of telling her to turn over the blue paper, you hand the folder to her. Ask her to open the folder to see which color smarties choose. (Remember, the folder says "Smarties always choose red.")

But what if she chooses purple? You just move to your next out, plan 3. Ask her to unroll her pointer. (Remember, the pointer says "Smarties always choose purple.")

So no matter what color she chooses, you have an out! That's the beauty of this trick. But you do need to remember where each out is. Blue starts with *b*, which reminds me to look on the back of the papers. Red starts with *r*, which reminds me to hand them the folder in my right hand. Purple starts with a *p*, which reminds me to open the pointer. Practice it right now so you can try it on one of your friends or a family member today, okay?

Roosevelt's Favorite Joke #15:
Q: What's a twip?
A: A twip is what a wabbit takes when he wides a choo-choo twain.

P Is for Patter

There are two parts to every magic trick—what you do and what you say. Most beginning magicians focus on the "do" part more than the "say" part. That's a mistake. But you're not going to make that mistake because you're a student of the famous (and handsome!) Roosevelt Rat. That means you're going to learn that what you say during an effect is just as important as learning the secret move.

Why is what you say so important? Because the story that you tell helps make the effect entertaining. And if an effect isn't entertaining, no one will watch it.

The story is so important that magicians have a special name for it. They call it **patter**. Lots of magicians do card tricks with key cards (see "K Is for Key Cards"), but they all use different patter. That's what makes magic so fun. Each magician can add his own unique twist to his tricks by making up his own patter.

So, let me give you a chance to make up some patter. Let's try to make up a version of the "Smart Cookie Test" just for you.

My Own Smart Cookie Test

What happens: The same thing as in the original Smart Cookie Test, only this time you make up the story.

What You Need: Let's stick with three colors of paper, a folder, and a pointer, just like before.

Secret: The secret is still outs, but *you get to decide what the outs will reveal*. For instance, you can tell your friend that there is one color that means you're cool or nice or funny. It can mean whatever you want it to mean. Think of something good and write it in the blank:

> There is one color that _____
> people always choose.

See, that wasn't so hard, was it? Now try to make it a little more interesting. If you wrote "cool" in the blank, try to think of a reason that each color would mean "cool." For instance, cool people always choose blue because blue is the color of the ocean, and the ocean is very cool.

Okay, now you try it. Make up a reason for each of the three colors:

> Blue: _____
>
> _____
>
> Purple: _____
>
> _____
>
> Red: _____
>
> _____

There, now you have your own personalized trick! Good work! I now promote you to a brown belt in rat magic. Use your power wisely.

Roosevelt's Favorite Joke #16:
Q: How can you tell when there's an elephant in your sandwich?
A: When it's too heavy to lift.

Q Is for Quick Cuts

Today I'm going to teach you a technique used in lots of card tricks. But before I do that, you need to know what "cutting the deck" means. "Cutting the deck" is this series of moves that you did in the "World's Smartest Rat" effect:

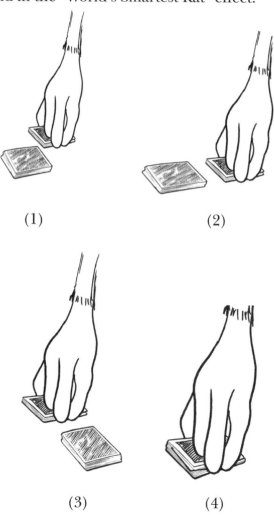

(1)   (2)

(3)   (4)

That's called cutting the deck. People do that to mix the cards up before a game of poker. It mixes the cards up by switching the top and bottom of the deck. But here's the important part—it doesn't mess up a key card. (If you don't remember what a key card is, review the "K Is for Key Card" lesson.)

So anytime you're doing a trick with a key card, you can let the audience cut the cards. In fact, you can let them cut the cards over and over again, as many times as they want! The key card will stay in position right on top of their chosen card.

Or, if you want to look like a professional card handler, you can cut the deck several times quickly yourself. We call these **quick cuts**. *They look impressive, but they don't affect the key card at all.*

New and Improved World's Smartest Rat

What happens: You invent a new animal that will find your friend's card. And you throw in some cool quick cuts.

What You Need: A deck of cards, a paper and pencil, and a good imagination.

Secret: You'll do this trick just like you did the original "World's Smartest Rat" effect in the "K Is for Key Card" lesson, but *now you can add quick cuts* to the effect. Just cut the deck several times after your friend puts her chosen card back in the deck. This will make it look even more impossible when you reveal her card. You can do the cuts yourself or you can let her do it; it doesn't matter.

Also, now that you know about patter, you can make improvements in what you say during the effect. Try to make it funnier by adding a joke to your patter. If you need ideas, check out a joke book from the library.

You can improve the story, too. Instead of using my picture, invent a new animal yourself. Maybe combine two animals and give it a funny name, like an owl and a dog (a "Hoot Dog"), or a centipede and a parrot (a "Walkie-Talkie"). Be creative and see what you can invent.

Star Tip: Now try this improved version of the effect out on a friend or a family member. I bet it will work a little better than it did before. Keep studying magic and you'll keep getting better and better at it, and that will make it more and more fun. That's true for any subject you study—it's hard at first, but if you stick with it, it will get easier and more fun, so don't give up!

Roosevelt's Favorite Joke #17:
Q: How many apples grow on a tree?
A: All of them.

R Is for Revelation

Good effects start with an interesting idea. We call that idea the **premise**. For example, the premise of the "Smart Cookie Test" is that smart people always pick a certain color. That interesting idea makes people want to pay attention to the effect.

Then, good effects have a **buildup**. That means they keep getting more interesting. In the "Smart Cookie Test," you make it more interesting by letting your friend take the test. That makes them really interested because she wants to see if she picked the right color.

Finally, good effects end with a big finish. In many cases, that surprise finish includes a revelation. A **revelation** is just a fancy way of saying that you revealed something. For example, in the "Smart Cookie Test" you reveal that "Smart cookies always choose blue." (Or purple or red, depending on which out you need to use—see "O Is for Outs.")

It's important to emphasize the revelation. Build up the excitement by saying, "You had three cards to choose from. In just a second, we'll find out if you chose the one right color." Wait a second, then turn the card around dramatically! Now that's a cool revelation!

Learn the following trick, and then try it out on someone. As you do, focus on making the revelation exciting.

Roosevelt Rat's Invisible Adventure

What happens: You write the names of different cartoon characters on pieces of paper and drop them in a shoebox. Your friend examines all the papers to make sure none of them say "Roosevelt Rat." You put the lid on the shoebox and I, Roosevelt Rat, sneak into the shoebox without anyone seeing me. (I'm so cool, huh?) I cross out one of the names and write my name on that sheet of paper. Finally, you open the shoebox and reveal the paper with my name on it.

What You Need: A shoebox, notebook paper, and pens. Before your friend comes over, prepare the papers: Cut five pieces of notebook paper into fourths. Write the name of a famous cartoon character in black ink on all but one of the papers: SpongeBob SquarePants, Scooby Doo, Mickey Mouse, Bugs Bunny, and Kim Possible. (Repeat the names so that four pieces of paper all say, "SpongeBob," etc., but only three pieces of paper say "Mickey Mouse.") Put them in the shoebox.

On the one leftover piece of paper, write "Mickey Mouse" in black ink. Then, in red ink, cross out "Mickey Mouse" and write "Roosevelt Rat." Keep the shoebox lid nearby, with this gimmicked piece of paper hidden under it.

Secret: *The gimmicked piece of paper will make the trick possible.* Invite your friend over and tell her that the incredibly amazing Roosevelt Rat has turned himself invisible. Pretend to show her your invisible rat by holding your hand out flat and "petting" the invisible rat. Your friend won't believe that you're really holding an invisible rat, but you will have her attention because an invisible rat is a good premise. Now you need to make it more interesting.

Bring out the shoebox with the papers in it. (You don't show the lid or the gimmicked paper yet.) Pull the papers out and let your friend examine them, front and back. Ask her to read them all and make sure none of them say "Roosevelt Rat" on them. Then ask her to put them in the box. Finally, you say, "Okay, we'll put the lid on the box and let you hold it to make sure nothing tricky happens." This is great misdirection because the trick is going to happen before you hand the box to her. In fact, the trick happens right while you're saying this.

As you pick up the lid, you also grab the gimmicked paper hidden underneath it. As you put the lid on the box, you let the hidden paper drop right into the box. Then you hand the box to your friend as you describe the invisible Roosevelt Rat sneaking into the box, writing his name on one of the pieces of paper, and sneaking back out. (That's the delay in this trick.)

Then ask your friend to open the box and look through the papers to see if Roosevelt was really there. The top piece of paper will be the gimmicked card that has "Mickey Mouse" crossed off and "Roosevelt Rat" written in. That's the revelation, and it's a good one. Try this effect soon!

Roosevelt's Favorite Joke #18:
Q: When is it polite to spit in someone's face?
A: When his moustache is on fire.

S Is for Self-Working

In many tricks, your hands do the secret move, like when you pretend to pick up a napkin to eat it but really you leave it in your other hand. That's called **sleight of hand.** Sleight is pronounced like "light," only with an "s" on the beginning, and it means "a trick." So "sleight of hand" is a trick you do with your hand.

Some tricks don't use any sleight of hand. They're called **self-working** tricks. *I like self-working tricks because there's no secret move.* You just memorize the patter and you're ready to go. Here's a good example of a self-working trick.

Choose Me!

What happens: Your friend chooses a square, then moves around to different squares, but always ends on the Roosevelt Rat square.

What You Need: The directions and the squares on page 77.

Secret: *This is a self-working trick.* All you need to do is explain to your friend that rats are everyone's favorite animal because they're so cute and cuddly. And smart. And ... Well, anyway, tell your friend that you'll prove it.

Then, read the directions on page 77 to him. You might have to explain that **wrapping around** is not allowed. In other words, you cannot go off one side of the board and then "wrap" around to the other side.

As long as he follows the directions, the trick will work. You don't have to practice any secret moves at all! Self-working tricks are nice, don't you agree?

Roosevelt's Favorite Joke #19:
Q: What did the frog say when the teacher asked him to name three famous poles?
A: North, South, and Tad.

Curtis Camel	Ruth Ann Reindeer	Trevor Trout	Petie Possum
Emily Eagle	Vicky Vulture	Sarah Songbird	Roosevelt Rat
Brent Beaver	Mackenzie Monkey	Dylan Dolphin	Susan Seahorse

Directions

1. Touch your finger to any shaded square.
2. Move left or right to the closest white square.
3. Move up or down to the closest shaded square.
4. Move diagonally to the closest white square.
5. Move left or right to the closest shaded square—that's your favorite animal in the whole world ... *Roosevelt Rat!*

T Is for Television

If you want to be a good magician, you should watch television. No, not *SpongeBob* or *Oprah*. You should watch magicians on television. And when you watch them, don't try to figure out how they do their tricks. Instead, watch to see how they make their effects interesting.

Good magicians work on their **showmanship**, which is the ability to present their effects in an entertaining way. Famous magicians have spent hours and hours developing their own style of showmanship. Think of Siegfried and Roy and their Bengal tigers. Or think of David Copperfield and his giant illusions, like making the Statue of Liberty disappear. Or picture the crazy stunts that David Blaine does, like being frozen in a giant ice cube.

When you see magicians on television, concentrate on their showmanship. Then work on your own showmanship. Here's one idea you can try out to make an effect more interesting: pretend it didn't work. If your friends insist that you just did a magic trick, deny it. Here, I'll show you what I mean.

The "I'm Not David Blaine" Effect

What Happens: You do a trick that David Blaine does on television, but you pretend it didn't work.

What You Need: A handful of coins and a permanent marker.

Secret: This trick uses the move you learned in the "Yummy Napkin" effect—the one where you pretend to grab a napkin but actually leave it in your other hand. *You combine misdirection with the idea of denying you're doing magic.* Here's how it works.

Take a handful of coins out of your pocket and show them to your friend. Do this with your left hand. Then ask her to pick one coin and to put a big *X* on it with the permanent marker. Finally, ask her to drop it back in your left hand with the other coins.

Then, use your right hand to pretend to take the marked coin. Don't really take it. Just close your left hand up at the same time so that your friend won't see the coin with the *X* still in your left hand. Use misdirection to make your friend think you really took the coin. Stare at your right hand as it moves away from your left. Hold your right hand up in front of your face as you say, "David Blaine does a trick on television where he makes a coin marked with an *X* disappear."

Then pretend to rub the coin on your right pant leg as you say, "All he does is rub it on his right pant leg. I guess he rubs it so hard that it completely disappears."

Then open your hand up so your friend can see it's empty. You pretend not to notice that the coin is gone. Just say, "I wish I knew how David Blaine does that, but I only know Roosevelt Rat tricks."

Your friend will probably be going crazy. She'll be saying, "The coin disappeared! Where did it go?" You just answer, "No, it didn't disappear. See, it's right here in my pocket with all the other coins."

Your friend will insist it traveled there magically, but you keep denying it. Say something like, "That would be so cool if I could make it travel there magically, but I don't know that trick."

Then your friend will say, "You must know the trick—you just did it!" You reply, "No, I wish I knew how do it, but I'm not David Blaine." And so on and so forth.

Notice what's happening. *Your friend is insisting you did magic.* She's trying to convince you that you're magical. Isn't that cool? Usually your friends try to figure the tricks out so they can prove you *didn't* do magic. This is just the opposite—they try to prove you *did* do magic! Try this showmanship trick out and see what you think.

Roosevelt's Favorite Joke #20:
Q: How many skunks does it take to make a big stink?
A: A phew.

U Is for Unconscious

Every day you make lots of decisions. You decide what clothes you'll wear, what you'll say to your friends, what books you'll read, and lots more. **Conscious** means you have to think about something, so we call these "conscious" decisions.

But there are lots of decisions you don't have to think about at all. These are called **unconscious** decisions. Your unconscious brain makes these decisions for you. Unconscious decisions include when to blink, when to breathe, how fast your heart should beat, and many others.

Some magic tricks take advantage of unconscious decisions. Here is one example.

Carrot Top

What Happens: You ask your mom and dad to name any vegetable and they pick the one that you wrote on a prediction slip.

What You Need: A pen and a piece of paper. Write "broccoli" on the paper and cross it out. Then write "corn" and cross that out, too. Finally, write "carrot" on the paper.

Secret: In this trick, *you take advantage of your parents' unconscious thoughts*. Here's how: First, you ask them a bunch of math questions. As soon as they answer the first question, ask them the second, then the third, and so on:

- What's 2 + 2?
- What's 4 + 4?
- What's 6 + 6?
- What's 8 + 8?
- What's 10 + 10?
- What's 12 + 12?

You immediately say, "Name a vegetable." They will probably answer, "Carrot." Then you turn your paper over and show your prediction.

You may be wondering what the addition questions have to do with vegetables. Well, those questions prepare your parents in two ways. First, those questions get your parents in the habit of answering quickly. And that makes them more likely to go with the first unconscious answer that pops into their head when you ask the vegetable question.

Secondly, the answer to the last math question is "24." When adults hear "24," they unconsciously think of 24-karat gold. (24-karat gold is gold that is 99 percent pure gold and only 1 percent other metals.) Since your parents are unconsciously thinking about 24-*karat* gold, they naturally think of carrots when you ask for a vegetable.

Star Tip: Since this trick depends on your parents' unconscious thoughts, it works about two out of three times. That means that one-third of the time your parents are going to guess a different vegetable. That's why we have two extra answers crossed out on the sheet. Maybe they'll guess broccoli or corn, and you can say, "Oh, I almost got it, but then I crossed that answer out." Your parents will still be impressed, so using three answers gives you a better chance of success.

Roosevelt's Favorite Joke #21:
Q: Where was Roosevelt Rat when the lights went out?
A: In the dark.

V Is for Vanish

Everyone expects a magician to be able to make objects **vanish**, or in other words, disappear. For example, a magician might put a quarter in his hand, snap his fingers, and open his hand, revealing that the quarter has vanished. Some magicians even vanish large objects, like real live elephants. David Copperfield vanished the Statue of Liberty once!

Since you probably don't own a Statue of Liberty, I'll teach you how to vanish a pencil and a quarter today. This is a classic. A **classic** is a trick that is so good that it never goes out of style.

Pencil and Quarter Vanish

What Happens: You try to vanish a quarter, but your pencil vanishes instead. When you finally find your pencil, then your quarter disappears.

What You Need: A pencil and a quarter.

Secret: *Misdirection is the key to this trick.* The pencil disappears while your audience is watching the quarter. Then the quarter disappears while your audience is looking for the pencil. It's so sneaky—I love it!

Here's what you do. Hold a quarter in your hand.
Bring up the pencil up to your ear, then swing it
down to tap the quarter as shown in these pictures:

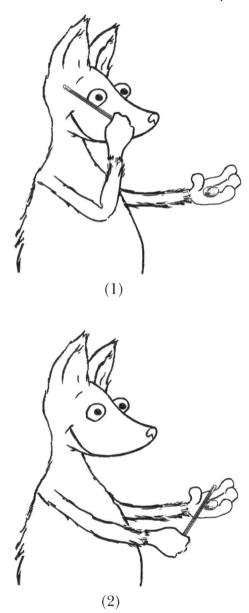

(1)

(2)

Do this three times, counting, "One, two, three." In between each tap, raise the pencil all the way up to your ear. On the third swing, actually leave the pencil behind your ear as shown in this picture:

On the third swing, pencil stays tucked behind your ear.

(3)

Drop the pencil off quickly so that you don't break the rhythm of your counting. Then look around, like you're searching for the pencil. This takes the audience completely by surprise because they were expecting the quarter to disappear!

Then say, "Oh, there it is," and turn your head so your audience can see the pencil. As you reach up to grab it from behind your ear, secretly drop the quarter into your pants pocket. That's great misdirection.

Then keep your left hand cupped so that it's not obvious the quarter is gone. Quickly count to three again with the pencil and open your hand to show the quarter has vanished. By this time, the audience has forgotten that they took their eyes off the quarter to look for the pencil. (You just used a delay.) So this trick uses misdirection and delay to create a surprising vanish. You're becoming a serious magician. Keep up the good work!

Roosevelt's Favorite Joke #22:
Q: The Eiffel Tower is tall, but what building has the most stories?
A: The library!

W Is for the Web

Today's magicians have a resource that wasn't available in the past. A **resource** is something or someone that you can learn from, like a book or a teacher. You can learn hundreds of magic tricks from this new resource—the World Wide Web.

The **World Wide Web** is made up of all the pages on the Internet that are connected together. You just click on a link and it takes you right to the page that you want. And the links on that page will take you to more pages, which will take you to more pages, and so on. Everything is connected together like a spiderweb, which is why it's called the World Wide *Web* and why most Internet pages start with "www."

The Web is a great place to learn new magic tricks. Today I'll teach you a trick I learned on the Web.

Lonely Kings

What Happens: Your friend deals out four piles of cards. The top card of each pile turns out to be a king. The second card of each pile is a queen.

What You Need: A deck of cards. Put all four queens on the top of the deck and then put all four kings on top of the queens. Now you have a **stacked deck**—a deck that is set up in a certain way for a trick.

Secret: *Once you have the deck stacked, this is a self-working trick.* Just give your friend the following directions and the trick will work itself. (Also, all the cards should be dealt facedown so that your friend can't see which cards they are until the end.)

1. Deal out about twenty cards into two piles. The first card goes into pile 1, the second goes into pile 2, then pile 1, pile 2, and so on.

2. Then pick up pile 1 and deal it into two new piles the same way. These piles will represent towns in the land of Astoria. So the first card goes into town 1, the second goes into town 2, then town 1, town 2, and so on.

3. Then pick up pile 2 and deal it into two new piles the same way. These will be town 3 and town 4. Now you have four "towns" with about five cards in each.

4. Please turn over the top card of each town and we'll see who the mayor of that town is. (The mayor of each town will be one of the kings that you set up earlier. Your friend will be surprised that he just happened to deal a king onto the top of each pile.)

5. The mayor would be very lonely if he didn't have a wife. Luckily, I have a feeling you dealt each mayor a wife, too. Please turn over the next card in each pile. (The next card will be the queen that you set up. Again, your friend will be amazed because he did all the dealing. It's neat when tricks make your friends feel special.)

That's just one example of a trick you can learn on the World Wide Web. If you want to learn more tricks from the Web, go to www.google.com and search for "magic tricks kids can do." Enjoy this free resource!

Roosevelt's Favorite Joke #23:
Q: What's black and white and red all over?
A: A zebra wearing too much lipstick.

X Is for eXplanation

Okay, so explanation doesn't really start with an *X*. Unfortunately, there are no magical xylophones or X-rays, so "eXplanation" will have to do.

Maybe that's a good thing, because your **explanation** of a trick is very important. Here's what I mean—suppose you're starting the "Lonely Kings" card trick. You don't want people to know that the deck is stacked, so how should you describe the deck? Here are your choices:

1. "Now I will take this deck, which is *not* stacked, and place it in your hands."

2. "Now I will take this *normal* deck and place it in your hands."

3. "Now I will take this *magical* deck, which possesses *strange* and *mysterious* powers, and place it in your hands."

Which of those explanations do you think will make people suspicious of the deck? If you're like most people, you probably guessed answer 3. That's wrong. (Sorry!) Actually, answers 1 and 2 cause suspicion. Why? Because people know you're trying to trick them, so they suspect everything you say is a lie.

If you say, "This deck is *not* stacked," they think it *is* stacked. If you say that it's a *normal* deck, they assume it's a **trick deck**. (A "trick deck" is a deck with gimmicked cards.) But if you say it's a *magical deck with strange and mysterious powers*, they assume it's a regular deck. I know that sounds backward, but that's how it works.

If you want people to ignore the deck, tell them it's magical. Now that you know this, you can start using your explanations to create even more misdirection. We'll use another classic trick as an example:

Crayon Confusion

What Happens: Your friend hands you a crayon behind your back. Without looking at it, you can tell its color.

What You Need: A box of crayons.

Secret: *You will use your explanation to throw your audience off track.* First, give your friend a box of crayons. Tell him that you have very sensitive fingers—so sensitive that you can feel the color of a crayon.

That's your explanation. The trick really does use your fingers, so you tell him your fingers have special powers. He'll assume you're trying to throw him off track, and he'll start looking for mirrors that help you see the crayon behind your back or he'll want to measure the crayons to see if they're different lengths.

With all the focus off your fingers, you're free to use them in the trick. So when your friend hands you a crayon behind your back, turn around and face him. Now he can't see the crayon. Take your right thumbnail and scrape off a little piece of crayon. Get it really stuck under your fingernail.

Then bring your right hand up to your forehead, like you need to concentrate. Leave the crayon behind your back in your left hand. As you bring your right hand up to your forehead, take a quick peek at the crayon sliver stuck in your thumbnail.

Now the rest is acting. Pretend to concentrate on the left hand as you try to "feel" the color of the crayon. If the color is purple, say, "It feels like a dark color. Maybe a blue, no … maybe a dark red … no, wait, now I recognize that texture—it's purple!"

Roosevelt's Favorite Joke #24:
Q: Which side of a rat has the most fur?
A: The outside.

Y Is for You Do as I Do

A "You Do as I Do" effect is like playing follow the leader or Simon says. You demonstrate what you want your friend to do, and she copies you exactly. This is a fun kind of effect because the audience gets to help you do the magic. The classic "You Do as I Do" effect is called, appropriately enough:

You Do as I Do

What Happens: You and a friend each get a deck. You both shuffle your deck, cut to a card, memorize it, and shuffle some more. Then you show each other the cards you cut to. It turns out that each of you cut to the same card!

What You Need: Two decks of cards.

Secret: The secret is a key card. This trick is very similar to the "World's Smartest Rat" effect in the "K Is for Key Card" lesson, except now your friend gets to help.

To begin this trick, let your friend choose which deck she wants to use. Then ask her to do everything you do. Begin by cutting your deck several times to mix it up. She should copy your moves.

Then tell your friend you want to make sure the decks are truly mixed up. Each of you should show your top card and make sure they don't match. Then each of you should show your bottom card and make sure they don't match either. This is important. Your friend's bottom card is the key card. Let's suppose it's the 2 of hearts. Memorize it and make sure that she puts it back on the bottom of her deck.

Now pull out one card from somewhere in the middle of your deck. Your friend should do the same. Don't show each other your cards. Ask your friend to memorize her card because she'll need to find it later. Don't bother memorizing the card you chose. Instead, make sure you still remember the bottom card of your friend's deck.

Now place your card facedown on top of your deck and have your friend do the same on hers. Give your decks another cut. Tell your friend that this cut is to make sure that each of your cards are lost somewhere in the middle of the deck. Actually, this brings the key card right on top of your friend's chosen card.

Now all that's left is the revelation. Here's how you do it. Switch decks with your friend, and ask her to look through your deck and take out the card that matches the one she chose. In other words, if she chose a 4 of diamonds, she should look for the 4 of diamonds in your deck. Have her pull the card out and set it facedown on the table.

At the same time, you look through the deck she gave you. You pretend to be looking for the card you chose, but actually you're looking for the key card. Look through the cards until you come to the key card, and your friend's card will be the one right in front of it.

Take this card and put it facedown on the table. Your friend puts her card down on the table, too. Finally, turn both cards over at the same time. Your friend will be shocked to see that you both just "happened" to choose the same card.

Roosevelt's Favorite Joke #25:
Q: Which animals can jump higher than the Eiffel Tower?
A: All of them. The Eiffel Tower can't jump.

96

Z Is for Zealous Mentor

This is our last lesson and my last chance to teach you the secrets of magic. But I don't want you to stop learning magic, so I'm going to help you find another teacher. I want you to find a zealous mentor.

Zealous means enthusiastic, and a **mentor** is a guide or teacher. So a zealous mentor is someone who is enthusiastic about guiding and teaching you. In this case, someone who is enthusiastic about teaching you magic.

So where do you find someone like that? A good place to start is your local magic store. Check the yellow pages to find a store close to you. Go to the magic store and tell them you want to buy a simple magic trick that costs less than ten dollars. Ask them to show you a couple tricks. They'll be happy to do it. Decide which one of those tricks you like the best and buy it. Then they'll teach you how to do the trick. If you buy a trick once a month, you'll keep getting better at magic, and you'll probably become friends with the staff at the store.

Another good place to find a mentor is an International Brotherhood of Magicians (IBM) ring or a Society of American Magicians (SAM) assembly. **Rings** and **assemblies** are just fancy names for clubs, so the IBM rings and SAM assemblies are clubs for magicians in your area. Usually they meet once a month to talk about and teach each other magic tricks. They would be delighted to have a young magician join their club. Go to their Web sites and look for a ring or assembly in your area:

- IBM—www.magician.org
- SAM—www.magicsam.com

Well, I'd say you know all the basics of magic now. So I'll say goodbye and teach you one last effect, which I learned at a magic store.

Amazing Book Test

What Happens: A **book test** is a magic trick where you predict which page of a book a friend will choose. You hand out a book and let several friends choose numbers. Then they add the numbers up and turn to that page in the book. Finally, you open your prediction and show that you had written down the first sentence of that page. Pretty cool, huh?

What You Need: A *Roosevelt Rat's Learn Magic from A to Z* book. You also need a pad of paper like you used in the "It All Adds Up" effect from the "G Is for Gimmick" lesson, a pencil, and an envelope. Look at page 21 and write down the first sentence on a piece of paper: "Here's what it looks like to your friend."

Put that paper in the envelope and seal it. Finally, on the back of your pad, write the numbers 8, 9, and 4. Don't flash these numbers.

Secret: *This trick uses a "force" to make sure your friends choose page 21.* A **force** is a trick that makes your friends think they have a free choice when they really don't. In this effect, your friends think they get to pick the page number, but they will always pick page 21. To force page 21, use the same method you did in the "It All Adds Up" effect from the "G Is for Gimmick" lesson.

To start, announce that you're going to do a book test. Have someone hold the prediction envelope. Ask three volunteers to write down a single-digit number on your pad. Then walk to the other side of the room and ask someone else to add up the numbers. As you move to the other side of the room, switch the pad to your other hand. This turns it over so that the numbers you wrote on the back are showing. These are the numbers the person adds up. That's how you force them to choose page 21.

Then ask someone to turn to page 21 in the book and read the first sentence. Ask someone else to open the sealed envelope and read the contents. Bow triumphantly and enjoy the look of amazement on your friends' faces.

Star Tip: I'd say you've earned your black belt in rat magic now. Use your new skill to have fun and entertain your friends. Remember that magic should make people laugh and make them wonder—it should never make people feel stupid or prove you're smarter than they are. Look for me, Roosevelt Rat, next time I come to your school. I want to hear which tricks you've tried and how they've worked.

Roosevelt's Favorite Joke #26:
Q: What do you call a fish with no eyes?
A: Fsh.

NIYT Is for Now It's Your Turn!

Did you know that reading this book is a form of exercise? Yes, it's true. Just like physical exercise strengthens the muscles in your body, reading strengthens the neurons and dendrites in your brain! (**Neurons** are the cells in your brain and **dendrites** are the wires that connect the neurons to each other. Each neuron can be connected to more than ten thousand other neurons by these dendrites!)

Now that you've read the whole book and strengthened the neurons and dendrites in your brain, I believe it's your turn to create some magic tricks. I want you to take the principles you've learned in this book, such as using an accomplice and misdirection and delay, and combine them in new ways to create your own magic tricks.

For example, maybe you want to perform an effect where you vanish a quarter from under a napkin. How would you do that? Could you use an accomplice?

Maybe you could put the quarter on your hand, cover it with the napkin, and ask a couple members of your audience to reach under the napkin and verify that the quarter is still there. Your accomplice could be the last person to check that the quarter is there and she could actually take the quarter away for you.

And could you add a delay to make it more convincing? Instead of pulling the napkin off right after your accomplice takes the quarter, tell a story about how this effect actually fooled the most famous magician of all, Harry Houdini! (That story is true, by the way.) Then, after everyone has forgotten that your accomplice even came near the quarter, slowly pull the napkin away and reveal the vanish!

Combining ideas to create new magic tricks is not easy, but it's great brain exercise! See what you can come up with. The following pages give you a format to record your new ideas so that you won't forget them. Good luck and happy creating!

Roosevelt Rat's Favorite Joke #27:
Q: What's black and white and makes a lot of noise?
A: A zebra with a drumkit.

Name of Effect: _____

What happens (short description):

_____
_____
_____
_____

What you need (list of supplies):

_____
_____
_____
_____

Secret (how the effect works):

_____
_____
_____
_____

Patter Ideas (what you say as you perform the effect):

_____
_____
_____
_____

Name of Effect: _____

What happens (short description):

_____
_____
_____
_____

What you need (list of supplies):

_____
_____
_____
_____

Secret (how the effect works):

_____
_____
_____
_____

Patter Ideas (what you say as you perform the effect):

_____
_____
_____
_____

Name of Effect: _____

What happens (short description):

_____

_____

_____

_____

What you need (list of supplies):

_____

_____

_____

_____

Secret (how the effect works):

_____

_____

_____

_____

Patter Ideas (what you say as you perform the effect):

_____

_____

_____

_____

Name of Effect: _____

What happens (short description):

_____

_____

_____

_____

What you need (list of supplies):

_____

_____

_____

_____

Secret (how the effect works):

_____

_____

_____

_____

Patter Ideas (what you say as you perform the effect):

_____

_____

_____

_____

Name of Effect: _____

What happens (short description):

_____
_____
_____
_____

What you need (list of supplies):

_____
_____
_____
_____

Secret (how the effect works):

_____
_____
_____
_____

Patter Ideas (what you say as you perform the effect):

_____
_____
_____
_____

Name of Effect: _____

What happens (short description):

_____
_____
_____
_____

What you need (list of supplies):

_____
_____
_____
_____

Secret (how the effect works):

_____
_____
_____
_____

Patter Ideas (what you say as you perform the effect):

_____
_____
_____
_____

Crossword Puzzle Review

Across

3. The time between when you do a secret move and the revelation
6. Someone who is "in" on the trick and helps you do it
8. Disappear
10. When you have a different plan for each choice your friend makes.

Down

1. Tricking the audience into looking at your left hand while you do the secret move in your right hand
2. Someone who teaches you a subject
4. To get rid of a gimmick
5. Tricks that don't require sleight of hand
7. When you accidentally show something you didn't want the audience to see
9. After you ditch the gimmick, you're _____

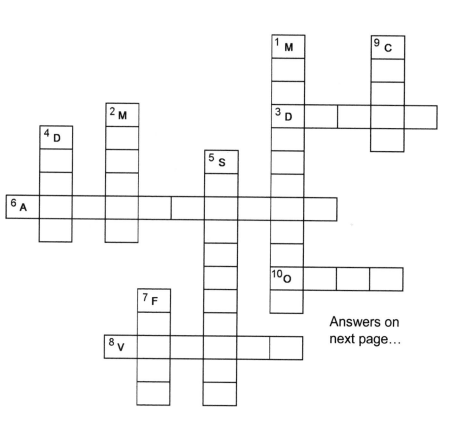

Answers on
next page…

Answers to Puzzle

Checklist

Effects I've Learned and Performed for Someone

- ❏ I "Red" Your Mind, 11
- ❏ Dog-Gone Prediction, 16
- ❏ "Have To" Make Money, 20
- ❏ Floating Cards, 24
- ❏ Hungry Hippo, 27
- ❏ Rat *Survivor*, 30
- ❏ It All Adds Up, 34
- ❏ The Flying Giraffe, 38
- ❏ Two-for-One Deal, 42
- ❏ Magical Pen, 44
- ❏ Unbeatable Gravity, 45
- ❏ World's Smartest Rat, 48
- ❏ Up, Up, and Away, 53
- ❏ The Yummy Napkin, 57
- ❏ Flipped-Out Coin, 61
- ❏ The Smart Cookie Test, 63
- ❏ My Own Smart Cookie Test, 66
- ❏ New and Improved World's Smartest Rat, 70
- ❏ Roosevelt Rat's Invisible Adventure, 73
- ❏ Choose Me!, 75
- ❏ The "I'm Not David Blaine" Effect, 78
- ❏ Carrot Top, 81
- ❏ Pencil and Quarter Vanish, 84
- ❏ Lonely Kings, 88
- ❏ Crayon Confusion, 92
- ❏ You Do as I Do, 94
- ❏ Amazing Book Test, 98
- ❏ Other: _____

Index of Terms